THE SHAPE OF BETTS MEADOW

A WETLANDS STORY

MEGHAN NUTTALL SAYRES
PICTURES BY JOANNE FRIAR

THE MILLBROOK PRESS   BROOKFIELD, CONNECTICUT

For Gunnar, Carrie and Finn,
and their children's children

Published by The Millbrook Press, Inc.
2 Old New Milford Road
Brookfield, CT 06804
www.millbrookpress.com

Library of Congress Cataloging-in-Publication Data
Sayres, Nuttall Meghan.
The shape of Betts Meadow / Meghan Sayres; illustrated
by Joanne Friar.—A Millbrook Press library ed.
p. cm.
Summary: A tract of land is returned to its natural state,
from pasture to wetland, as streams are unblocked, animals move back in, and native plants grow.
ISBN 0-7613-2115-2 (lib. bdg.)
1. Wetland restoration—Washington (State)—Betts
Meadow—Juvenile literature. 2. Restoration ecology—
Washington (State)—Betts Meadow—Juvenile literature.
3. Betts Meadow (Wash.)—Juvenile literature. [1. Wetland
restoration. 2. Restoration ecology. 3. Wetland ecology.
4. Ecology. 5. Betts Meadow (Wash.)] I. Friar, Joanne H.,
ill. II. Title.
QH76.5.W2 S28 2002 333.91'8153'097923—
dc21 2001037069

Author's Note

Lavinia Holmquist and her son, Gunnar, decided one day to nurture a
small piece of land. They thought of it as their gift back to the Earth. Lavinia gathered
together a large part of her savings to buy Betts Meadow, a 140-acre dry pasture, ringed
with a forest of tall, old pine trees. It was a beautiful place, but it seemed that it had been
changed from what it had once been: a wetland. Gunnar, a medical doctor, soon became a
wetland doctor.

Gunnar put aside his stethoscope, picked up his camera, and took photographs of Betts
Meadow. These photos showed that about a hundred years ago three streams had coursed
through the meadow, and beavers had been at work there. Later, someone had blocked the
streams to dry out the land for cattle to graze. Many species of plants and animals left with
the water.

This poem is the story of Betts Meadow after Lavinia and Gunnar Holmquist made their
decision to take care of it.

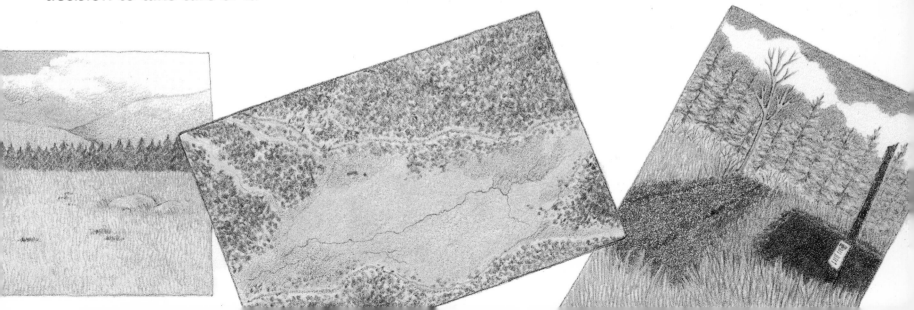

One soft, fine day
a doctor named Gunnar
bought a meadow called Betts.

This land was as dry
as an old cowpie, empty
of critters—even the coyote.

"Every meadow deserves a drink," declared Gunnar to his dogs, Hoagie and Zoe.

So he traded his stethoscope
for:

one bulldozer
one dragline crane and ...

one fact-finding flight high above Betts Meadow.

Inside a plane, engines
rumbled and rattled Gunnar's
ears and rump
as he mapped
grand old streams
that once watered this land.

Then Gunnar dug deep ponds.
Like a hungry earthworm
his bulldozer burrowed.

Dust clung to Gunnar's mustache.
Grit tickled his teeth and throat.

Like a giant metal dragon,
his dragline crane

gnawed and clawed
and belched black smoke

loosening banks
of mountain streams
that once tumbled through the meadow.

Drip by drop,
water trickled
this way
and that way

down
the hillside
chock-full of cheat grass.

Winter snow
and spring rain
helped the streams fill his ponds.

Gunnar planted pine saplings,
and poured four-inch
cutthroats

that speckled
in pebbled shadows.

He sprinkled in every inch
of his meadow
wildflower seeds that ...

bloomed pink, white, and blue in June.

Then,
seven kinds of sedge:

soft
smooth
and sawbeaked
settled beside cheat grass.

Pondweed wallowed below water lilies
that sunbathed on the surface.
Cattails, rooted in marsh mud,
sent shoots to the stars.

Dayglow tree frogs fed on mosquitoes.

Beavers built
dams with branches
in streambeds that rambled.

Daredevil kingfishers
dappled and darted
cackling, "RAAACK, rack,
rack, rack, rack."

Elk bugled love notes,
nuzzled in buttercups
and touch-me-nots.

Footfalls of cougars
kept company with bears.

Betts Meadow is empty and thirsty no more.
If someday you come and hike to the hilltop,
you will see what Gunnar has shaped—

together with the wind,
the rain, and the sun.

Wetland Plants and Animals
Living in Betts Meadow

algae, bacteria, fungi: See **microbes**

beavers: Beavers have done more for wetlands than any other mammal. They build dams, which help create natural ponds. They build with grass or mud and wood, from saplings to huge Aspen trees. Beavers plaster dam leaks with mud and roots. They will raise their dams to keep up with incoming water and sediment. When dams are blown out by floods, they rebuild them. Beavers are dependent on wetlands for survival. They eat tubers, or buds on the stems of plants and tree bark.

buttercups: Several kinds of buttercups live in wetlands and uplands. The western buttercup lives in moist meadows and blooms from April to July with small yellow flowers. White water buttercups live in ponds, pools and ditches and bloom form May to August. Its flowers are white with yellow stamens.

cattails: Cattails are one of the most common wetland plants. They are able to live in soil with little oxygen. Cattails take oxygen from the water and soil and send it to its foliage. Cattails provide cover for amphibians and birds and other smallcreatures. Muskrats use cattails to construct their homes. Cattail roots contain sweet edible starch. Muskrats, beavers, and deer, elk, and moose like the energy-filled tubers of cattails.

cheat grass: One of the most common of the wild grasses that grow in the West.

coyotes: Coyotes are not dependent on wetlands, but like other animals such as cougars, foxes, and raccoons, they enjoy the abundance of waterfowl, eggs, and other wildlife found in a wetland.

cutthroat trout: Cutthroat trout are colorful fish with pink stripes and black dots. They feed on insects and crustaceans. They spawn from March to July. Kokanee salmon and eastern brook trout compete with them for zooplankton—microscopic food. In the streams above Betts Meadow, the eastern brook trout had pushed out the cutthroat. This is why Gunnar chose to reintroduce, or bring back, the Westslope cutthroat to Betts Meadow.

elk: Elk are not dependent on wetlands, but like other large herbivores such as deer and moose, they enjoy the abundance of grasses that grow in and near wetlands.

kingfishers: These "feathery fishermen" are flying predators of wetlands. They are small birds that dive for fish.

microbes: Microscopic organisms such as bacteria, algae, fungi, and protozoa attach to the roots of wetland plants where oxygen has leaked out of the plants. These organisms "eat up" waste or contaminants that come in contact with them. The contaminant is turned into food for the microorganism at the same time the water is purified or cleaned. The microbe is also food for other wetland inhabitants farther up the food chain.

pondweed: This plant provides food and cover for freshwater wetland inhabitants. It produces seeds and tubers, which are eaten by ducks, geese, and fish. The plant also lives underwater and helps to oxygenate the water.

sedge: This common freshwater plant lives above and below the water. Sedge sends oxygen from the air down to its roots, which are embedded in the soil. Sedge helps with water purification. Oxygen in its roots leaks into the spaces around the roots. Microscopic organisms (microbes) attached to the roots benefit from the oxygen.

tree frogs: Tree frogs find shelter in wetland grasses. They lay their eggs on living and dead underwater plants. Many of the 2,600 species of frogs live in wetlands. Few frogs lived in Betts Meadow when Gunnar first began work on his ponds. Today they are so numerous they keep him awake at night when he camps there.

water lilies: Water-lily roots float below the surface, while their large, flat leaves and white flowers float on top of the water. The plants provide food and cover for wetland wildlife and perches for birds.

What Is a Wetland?

A wetland is a place where water meets land: bogs, marshes, swamps, estuaries, and bays. Wetlands can be low-lying land where the underground water rises to the surface. Wetlands include the places where rivers meet oceans. They can contain freshwater, salt water, or both.

Wetlands receive, hold, and recycle nutrients continually washed in from higher ground. These nutrients support many species of wildlife, including vegetation that cannot be seen without a microscope, that provide food for fish, amphibians, crustaceans, insects, birds, animals, and people. Wetlands are the most productive ecosystems on Earth.

Some wetlands are inhabited year-round. Others are visited seasonally when fish spawn or when migratory birds stop to rest. Some are visited daily by creatures that come to drink, forage, and hunt for food.

Wetlands are the most threatened wildlife and fishery habitats of all our natural resources. Some 200 million acres of wetlands existed in the continental United States before colonization. Less than half remain. International organizations, federal agencies, scientists, developers, and environmentalists have just begun to work together to protect the world's wetlands.

Where to Write for More Information:

Sierra Club
330 Pennsylvania Avenue, S.E.
Washington DC 20003

The Nature Conservancy
1815 North Lynn Street
Arlington, VA 22209

The Wilderness Society
900 Seventeenth Street, N.W.
Washington, D.C. 20006-2596

Society for Ecological Restoration
1207 Seminole Highway
Madison, WI 53711

National Institute for Urban Wildlife
10921 Trotting Ridge Way
Columbia, MD 21044

The Children's Rainforest
P.O. Box 936
Lewiston, Maine 04240

National Audubon Society
950 Third Avenue
New York, NY 10022

Internet Sources

"Wetlinks"

References/ Additional Reading

Creating Freshwater Wetlands, by Donald A. Hammer, Lewis Publishers, 1996.
Saving Our Wetlands, by Karen Liptak, Franklin Watts, 1991.
Disappearing Wetlands, by Helen J. Challand, Childrens Press, 1992.
Earth Ponds, A Country Pond Maker's Guide to Building, Maintenance, and Restoration, by Tim Matson, Countryman Press, 1982, 1991.
WOW! The Wonders of Wetlands, An Educators Guide, The Watercourse, 201 Culbertson Hall, Montana State University, Bozeman, MT 59717.

Acknowledgments

Every story has its circle of friends and especially this one. I would like to thank Gunnar Holmquist and his wife Carrie Lipe for sharing Betts Meadow with my family and for helping with wetland facts and sources.

Special thanks to Patricia Nikolina Clark, Mary Farrell, Claire Rudloph Murphy, Mary Douthitt, Marie Whalen and my editor, Amy Shields, for their suggestions on this manuscript.

Contributions from the sale of this book will help maintain wetland restoration projects such as this one.